AIR COMMAND AND STAFF COLLEGE
AIR UNIVERSITY

I0447199

Strategic Implications of Culture

Historical Analysis of China's Culture and Implications for United States Policy

KIMBERLY A. CRIDER
Major, USAFR

Air Command and Staff College
Wright Flyer Paper No. 8

MAXWELL AIR FORCE BASE, ALABAMA

September 1999

Disclaimer

Opinions, conclusions, and recommendations expressed or implied within are solely those of the author and do not necessarily represent the views of Air University, the United States Air Force, the Department of Defense, or any other US government agency. Cleared for public release: distribution unlimited.

Foreword

It is my great pleasure to present another of the Wright Flyer Papers series. In this series, Air Command and Staff College (ACSC) recognizes and publishes the "best of the best" student research projects from the prior academic year. The ACSC research program encourages our students to move beyond the school's core curriculum in their own professional development and in "advancing aerospace power." The series title reflects our desire to perpetuate the pioneering spirit embodied in earlier generations of airmen. Projects selected for publication combine solid research, innovative thought, and lucid presentation in exploring war at the operational level. With this broad perspective, the Wright Flyer Papers engage an eclectic range of doctrinal, technological, organizational, and operational questions. Some of these studies provide new solutions to familiar problems. Others encourage us to leave the familiar behind in pursuing new possibilities. By making these research studies available in the Wright Flyer Papers, ACSC hopes to encourage critical examination of the findings and to stimulate further research in these areas.

John W. Rosa, Brig Gen, USAF
Commandant

Preface

I wanted to research and write a paper that will provide a culturally based view of social and political change and the strategic implications those changes might have on international relations and, specifically, military policy and planning. It is my hope that this research will give policy makers and planners cause to consider carefully the important underlying cultural factors that inevitably influence the strategic goals and behaviors of nations as they respond to a dynamic contextual environment and interact with each other on the global stage.

I wish to acknowledge and thank my research advisor, Dr. Abigail Gray-Briggs, for her assistance in helping me develop this research topic and for her insightful guidance in crafting this paper. I also want to thank Dr. Kathleen Mahoney-Norris and Dr. Tim Castle for sharing their expertise in political science and strategic area studies and for providing me with their intellectual counsel as I explored and developed this research topic.

Abstract

In today's dynamic and multipolar strategic environment there is a heightened potential for greater conflict. One reason for this lies in the different ways in which state and nonstate actors interpret and respond to the myriad challenges and op-portunities of a much more turbulent global context. These dif-ferences in interpretation and response are largely rooted in dif-ferences in culture, for it is culture that forms the subconscious set of shared meanings that guide group behaviors and percep-tions. Understanding culture in terms of the deep, underlying assumptions and shared mind-sets held by both state and non-state actors is critical for today's strategic military planner in attempting to predict the potential for conflict and in planning for effective conflict resolution.

In this paper, the author uses Mary Douglas's group-grid ty-pology model for framing culture to describe the strategic impli-cations of culture and culture's response to a changing global context. The author then applies these concepts to analyze the effect of cultural change in China and its implications for cur-rent and future US-China relations. Through this analysis, the author reveals important differences in cultural perspective be-tween China and the United States. These cultural differences encourage different solutions to the common strategic problems of security and prosperity and, thus, potentially cause misper-ceptions and dangerous miscalculations in policy. Long-term strategic cooperation with China requires that US planners and policy makers understand these cultural differences and factor them into every realm of engagement with China.

Strategic Implications of Culture

Historical Analysis of China's Culture
and Implications for United States Policy

Leaders of the world's nations today face a common challenge: how to ensure their nations' security and prosperity in a world that has become increasingly dynamic and uncertain. While the problems of national security and prosperity may be similarly shared, the solutions selected to solve these problems may in fact be very different. Solutions vary because the ways people perceive and respond to opportunities and challenges are influenced in large degree by what Glen Fisher refers to as "culturally-established mental frameworks or mindsets."[1] These mind-sets—based on established cultural beliefs, values, and biases—elicit different means of evaluating events, different decision-making frameworks, and different objectives which could all have positive or negative effects on international relations.[2] Fisher asserts that anyone concerned with international affairs needs to understand the ways in which these mind-sets affect them and those they are interacting with, if they intend to build alliances and partnerships to sustain regional and global stability.[3]

This assertion is particularly important for United States (US) policy makers and military planners engaged in efforts to "shape the international environment and create conditions favorable to US interests and global security."[4] This key step in the strategic approach to both the US National Security Strategy and National Military Strategy requires that the United States exert global leadership in partnering with other countries around the world to deal with the challenges and opportunities presented by today's uncertain security environment. Shaping the international environment implies, therefore, the need to develop an appreciation of culture and how culturally based mind-sets influence the solutions that may be selected by actors around the world to respond to common security and prosperity challenges. Understanding these concepts as they relate to US National Security Strategy and National Military Strategy objectives is critical for both policy makers and military planners as a way to predict the potential for conflict as well as to plan effective strategies to preclude future conflict.

Unfortunately, an appreciation of the sociocultural factors that influence the actions of nations are not often included in the planning efforts of US diplomats and military strategists. As Paul M. Belbutowski asserts, "Culture, comprised of all that is vague and intangible, is not generally integrated into strategic planning except at the most superficial levels."[5] A lack of this type of understanding can lead to serious misperceptions and miscalculations in policy which, as Jack S. Levy warns, have historically been factors in the outbreak of war.[6]

This paper helps to rectify this weakness in US strategic planning by first presenting a working definition of culture based on the current thinking of social anthropologists. The author explores Fons Trompenaar's definition of culture as a means for solving problems, Edgar Schein's model for describing culture, and a theoretical concept of culture as the way of life a group of people chooses to follow. That way of life provides the basis for the shared values, beliefs, biases, and accepted patterns of social relations among a culture's constituent members.

Next, the author introduces the group-grid analysis model developed by Mary Douglas as a means of explaining four common organizing principles found in cultures throughout the world. Using this model, the author explores Douglas's four primary typologies for differentiating culture, examines how and why cultures may transition along the continuum between each typological extreme, and considers the strategic implications for conflict that may occur in cultures experiencing transition.

Following this discussion, the author applies the definition of culture and the group-grid analysis model to a historical analysis of China's culture. China provides a rich opportunity for cultural study for several reasons. The culture of China is the world's oldest existing culture. China's culture is greatly unified, allowing a broad-based analysis using the definition of culture and group-grid typology framework described in this paper. Chinese culture remains largely homogeneous, although change has occurred throughout the centuries and important subcultures have gained prominence in recent years, adding intriguing dimensions to the analysis. Moreover, China's renewed economic strength, booming population, and increasing influence in the Asia-Pacific region have made more cooperative relations with the United States a key aspect of the US National Security Strategy. Understanding Chinese culture, including its historical underpinnings and pressures for change, allows US policy makers and military planners to more clearly compre-hend how China responds to the common challenges of security and prosperity in today's uncertain strategic environment. With the insight developed using the cultural lens crafted and ap-plied in earlier sections, this paper concludes with a culturally based analysis of current US-China relations, particularly with regard to the issue of broader democratization in China and the implications for long-term strategic cooperation.

Defining Culture

Culture is often overlooked in military strategic planning and diplomatic policy making because by its very nature culture is largely hidden from everyday awareness. It is nevertheless om-nipresent, subconsciously guiding the behavior, choices, and interactions of its constituent members. This section sheds a light on the elusive nature of culture and offers a working defi-nition of culture based on a survey of several of the most current writings and theories regarding sociocultural phenomena.

Trompenaar's assertion that culture is like gravity, "you do not experience it until you jump six feet in the air," [7] is a compel-ling metaphor when one considers that the only time cultural biases are apparent is when one attempts to do something in contradiction to that bias. When it comes to effective interna-tional relations and military strategic planning; however, it is particularly imprudent to delay one's appreciation of cultural biases among would-be allies and strategic partners until the potentially disastrous occurrence of a cultural faux pas.

One approach to a more tangible understanding of culture is to think about it as "the way in which a group of people solves problems."[8] The word "culture" is derived from the same root as the verb "to cultivate," meaning to till the soil. Culture, like cultivating, implies a way in which people act upon nature to solve common problems.[9] Trompenaar asserts culture, at its essence, "is nothing more than the way in which groups have organized themselves over the years to solve the problems and challenges presented to them" in the most effective way possible.[10]

Central to understanding the elusive yet encompassing na-ture of culture and its affect on human decisions and behavior is Schein's model, which depicts culture in three layers.[11] The most basic assumptions about existence, how to cope with the problems of daily life, and how to perceive, think, and feel in relation to those problems are hidden deep in a group's subconscious, forming the very core of its culture. These basic assumptions are manifested in more explicit ways in terms of the shared norms a group holds about what is right or wrong and what is good and bad. Norms and values reside at what Schein calls the middle layer of culture. The most explicit manifestations, at the outer layer of culture, are the more obvious factors such as language, dress, artwork, social structures, and government systems.

Implicit in Schein's model is the concept from Michael Thompson, Richard Ellis, and Aaron Wildavsky's work on cultural theory[12] that states culture encompasses "the total way of life of a people, their interpersonal relations as well as their attitudes."[13] Thompson, Ellis, and Wildavsky provide three important concepts that further support understanding of culture and emphasize the importance of Schein's middle layer of culture—cultural bias, social relations, and ways of life. Cultural bias refers to shared values and beliefs. Using the Schein model described earlier, shared values and beliefs, or the ideals a group holds about what is right and wrong, are usually found at the middle layer of culture. Social relations are patterns of interpersonal relations and fall into the category of norms also found at the middle layer of culture. Cultural biases and social relations are based on underlying assumptions about how to solve life's basic problems and are made explicit in specific behaviors and structures. A way of life, according to Thompson, Ellis, and Wildavsky, refers to "a viable combination of social relations and cultural bias."[14]

Social relations and cultural biases, indeed norms and values, ideally exist in a reciprocal, mutually reinforcing state. Therefore, just as "cultures become unstable when the norms do not reflect the values of a group," social relations and cultural biases must support each other for a way of life to remain viable. [15]

Thompson, Ellis, and Wildavsky refer to this phenomenon as the "compatibility condition," arguing that "a way of life will remain viable only if it inculcates in its constituent individuals the cultural bias that justifies it."[16] A lack of compatibility between shared values and the social relations they help legitimatize is the basis for how ways of life fail to maintain themselves over time and thus leads to cultural change—a subject analyzed in more detail and then applied to China later in this paper. Central to understanding cultural change and the implications for potential conflict is an assessment of what happens at the middle layer of culture to cause incompatibility between the established cultural biases and patterns of social relations that make a way of life no longer viable for its membership.

For the purposes of this paper, culture is defined as a way of life based upon a shared set of meanings that people use when confronted with problems to "interpret their experience and guide their action."[17] This definition is derived from the follow- ing operating premises. First, the most basic assumptions about how to cope with life's problems are hidden deep at cul- ture's core, guiding reactions and solutions in a subconscious but powerful way. Second, these underlying meanings are manifested in certain cultural biases (i.e., values) and patterns of social relations. Third, a way of life (i.e., culture) is considered viable by its membership when there is compatibility between what people value and how people interact with one another in the normal pattern of social relations.

What can US policy makers and military planners take away from this definition of culture? Belbutowski writes that today, "more than ever, a sense of vision is required for senior leaders and policy makers to estimate the intangible forces [of culture] at work in the environment within which the United States will have to function into the 21st century."[18] In today's complex and dynamic international environment, different cultures may apply different meanings to the problems presented to them. Those meanings may in turn drive potentially disparate solu- tions that could lead to misunderstandings and create the basis for violence and conflict.

Thus, one culture's strategy for ensuring its security and stability in a complex and unstable world may be geopolitical isolation and strict internal control via one-party rule. Within this cultural way of life, the strict patterns of social control dictated by the one-party system are legitimized by an over- arching bias in favor of stability for the collective good. China has, for example, followed this type of strategy for much of the last century. The United States, on the other hand, seeks secu- rity by promoting democracy, open market economies, and its own values throughout the globe. The way of life for American culture is biased toward more individual autonomy and loose patterns of social relations that afford individual freedom of choice as its solution for stability. Clearly, these strategies are dichotomous and can lead to misperceptions, mistrust, and potential conflict. To be effective in developing cooperative international relations, senior leaders, planners, and policy makers responsible for US national security must develop an appreciation for culture and its importance in driving different and sometimes conflicting solutions to common geopolitical problems.

Group-Grid Typology: A Model for Differentiating Culture and Understanding Culture Change

Developing practical insight into the nature of culture requires that US leaders have not only a working definition of culture but also an understanding of how to examine cultures using a typological construct, how cultural change occurs within the construct, and the strategic implications of those changes in culture.

As previously discussed, social anthropologists generally agree that in every culture, "a limited number of universally shared human problems need to be solved. One culture can be distinguished from another by the specific solutions it chooses for those problems."[19] Where the researchers tend to disagree, however, is in how those universally shared problems are conceptualized. In the literature on the subject, two dimensions of common problems appear to cut across the various studies and surveys. These two dimensions are the relationship between the individual and the group (or individualism versus collectivism) and the relationship to authority (or rules versus relationships). One researcher, Mary Douglas, offers a typology based on these two dimensions that provides a useful way for differentiating cultures.

Douglas asserts that group and grid are two dimensions of sociality that can adequately capture the variability of an individual's involvement in social life.[20] The group dimension is the extent to which individuals see themselves as members of a group and therefore act in accordance with group norms (collectivism). Within this dimension, the higher the group rating, the more individuals are willing to sacrifice their own interests for the welfare of the group. High-group societies find people linked together in "common residence, shared work, shared resources and recreation."[21] The grid dimension denotes the degree of social regulation and stratification. Douglas describes a high-grid social context as one in which "an explicit set of institutionalized classifications keeps [individuals] apart and regulates their interactions."[22] In this setting, strict rules and lines of authority are established and definitive roles separate men from women, fathers from sons, rulers from peasants. Cultures with a low-grid rating have less definitive separations as individuals are "increasingly expected to negotiate their own relationships with others."[23] For further explanation, see figure 1 below.

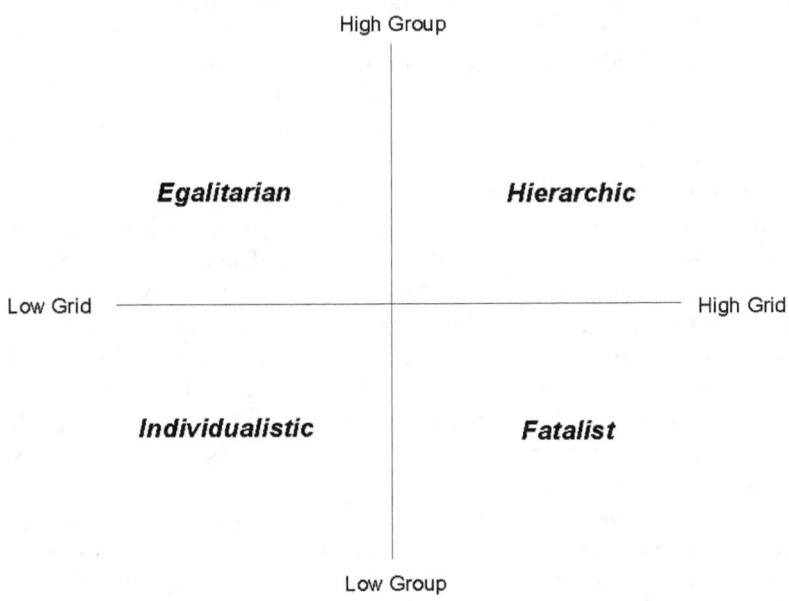

Figure 1. Group-Grid Typology

Taken together, the two dimensions of the group-grid framework define four basic ways of life: hierarchy, egalitarianism, individualism, and fatalism. Thompson, Ellis, and Wildavsky maintain that these four ways of life each meet the "conditions of viability"—meaning that each is distinguished from another by a certain pattern of social relations that supports and is supported by very specific shared values and beliefs. [24] Earlier, we defined culture as a way of life based on a shared set of meanings for solving life's problems and manifested in a specific pattern of social relations and shared cultural biases (values and beliefs). Cultures are considered viable ways of life by their membership when the patterns of social relations are compat-ible with the group's values and beliefs. In each of the four basic ways of life defined by the group-grid model, there is a set of social relations compatible with certain values and beliefs. This pattern and its complementary biases are the basis for differen-tiating one way of life from another.

Hierarchies are characterized by strong group boundaries and binding social prescriptions. Individuals in this social con-text are bound both by group norms and socially imposed roles. Authority is legitimized on the grounds of accepted social strati-fication and the belief that "different roles for different people enable people to live together more harmoniously than alterna-tive arrangements." [25]

Egalitarian environments are distinguished by strong group boundaries with minimal prescriptions regarding social regula-tion. Egalitarians place a high degree of value on the equality of each individual member of the group. Because these types of groups lack internal role differentiation and no individuals hold positions of authority from which to exercise control over oth-ers, conflict resolution can be very difficult. Decision making can be a lengthy process as the group strives for consensus. With no named authority figures, relations among members can be ambiguous at best.

In individualistic societies, all boundaries are temporary and subject to change and negotiation. Self-regulation is the governing norm as individuals are neither bound by group norms nor prescribed roles. Individuals in such environments seek power by negotiating profitable relationships with others. Democracies and free-market societies are examples of this type of social context.

People who find themselves excluded from group membership and bound by strict regulations or role separations typify the fatalistic way of life. Like hierarchists, fatalists have little indi-vidual autonomy. Their decisions about how they spend their time, with whom they associate, what they wear, and where they work are strictly controlled. Yet, unlike hierarchists, fatalists live in social isolation, "excluded from membership in the group responsible for making the decisions that rule their life." [26]

One can use the Douglas model to differentiate one group's culture from another. Most important, however, the model provides insight into how cultural change occurs and the im - plications of those changes for both domestic and interna - tional relations.

Indeed today, more than ever, cultures exist in a dynamic, information-rich global environment, making change inevitable. Cultural change occurs when an existing way of life is no longer viable and a new way of life emerges to replace it. As mentioned earlier, cultural theory posits that a way of life will endure only if it can continuously instill certain values and beliefs, and in - culcate a supporting pattern of social relations to sustain it. When this occurs, a way of life with its accompanying shared values and social relations provides its adherents with "the fab - ric of meaning," that is, the necessary and appropriate solutions for life's problems. [27] Changes in culture happen when "people realize that certain old ways of doing things do not work any more." [28]

Cultural change is usually not sudden since values and be - liefs hidden at the subconscious middle layer of culture are difficult to influence directly. But change can and will occur "when successive events intervene in such a manner as to pre - vent a way of life from delivering on the expectations it has generated, thereby prompting individuals to seek more promis - ing alternatives." [29] A useful analogy to this process is found in science. [30] Scientific theories lose their adherents when a signifi - cant amount of successive anomalies build up against those theories. As real-world evidence mounts, doubts build and de - fections follow. "A persistent pattern of surprises forces indi - viduals to cast around for alternative ways of life (or theories) that can provide a more satisfying fit with the world as it is." [31]

While gradual, cultural change can occur in several divergent directions, making a change much more difficult to control and producing potentially undesirable effects. Douglas's research shows that given the four ways of life in the group-grid typology, shifts may occur in up to three different and potentially simul - taneous directions—along the group dimension, along the grid dimension, and diagonally. [32] Thus, replacing a hierarchic social system with a more individualistic one (such as democracy) is not simply a direct shift from hierarchy to individualism. This type of change often brings with it accompanying or intermediate changes that may produce some unexpected or undesirable side effects.

One possible accompanying or intermediate change in a move from hierarchy to individualism is a shift down the grid dimension from stratified relationships to more equality in social status. This change represents a shift toward egalitarianism. Some individuals may want their society to move in this direction, believing that authoritative institutions and social stratifications create too much disparate privilege between the haves and have-nots. US policy makers and military strategic planners should note that such frustration has fueled the idealist aspirations of many socialist reform movements, including those which helped to drive Mao Tse-tung's Cultural Revolution in China.

Problems with this type of change can lead, however, to increased domestic conflict that has subsequent effects. For instance, the problems associated with egalitarian systems (lack of internal role differentiation, arduous conflict resolution, and lengthy decision-making processes) may frustrate the leaders of large egalitarian societies who find it difficult to maintain order without strict social regulation and therefore revert to the higher-grid orientations that worked so well in the past. This may have been the case in China when, after the Cultural Revolution, the cadre leadership formed to become the new elite governing body on behalf of the masses. As John King Fairbank argued in 1974, despite Mao's revolution, China did not free itself from its hierarchical Confucianist past. [33]

A second possible change step, which may occur simultaneous to or independent of other changes in a move from hierarchy to individualism, is a shift down the group dimension from collective interests to individualized ones. When the change favors greater individualism with no increase in autonomy, it is a move toward fatalism. In this situation, group membership no longer provides a safety net for individuals at the bottom strata. Each individual is left to his or her own devices and resources. Some will get by while others will find themselves powerless and socia lly isolated in a seemingly uncaring world. The inevitable, albeit unintended, consequence of increased fatalism in any push toward greater individualism presents a strong destabilizing social tension. As self-seeking interests are zealously pursued, expectations are raised to the point that many must be repressed by strict control mechanisms to preclude a degeneration into lawlessness and anarchy. Those finding themselves among the newly disenfranchised fatalists in a transitioning culture may wonder if the promise of liberalization is really worth it, and may desire a return to the days when they were not outcasts but members of the larger social sphere. For example, when the regime in modern China began reforming its urban economy in the 1980s through increased decentralization and commercialization, "[it] released strong entrepreneurial impulses all over China."[34] Today, however, "between 30-200 million people in China are in search of employment, encamping in and around temporary cities and creating a potentially volatile pool of poor and discontented citizens."[35] These obvious destabilizing side effects "make the vast majority of Chinese (both outside and inside the power structure) worried about the dangers of chaos . . . and most therefore go along with the current emphasis to preserve stability."[36]

In the examples discussed above, cultural change wrought serious consequences that caused those in power to reconsider the value of the change and to attempt to lessen the destabilizing effects by reverting to old, familiar cultural biases and social patterns. These examples also demonstrate the utility of the group-grid typology as a model not only to describe cultures in terms of their particular biases and social patterns but, more important, to assess the potential side effects that may occur when cultural change is initiated. The potential for cultural destabilization must be carefully considered both by domestic leaders attempting internal change and would-be international partners who may wish to influence change within another culture.

The remaining sections of this paper provide a more detailed analysis of China's culture. Using the group-grid typology, the author explores the nature of China's historically predominant way of life (in terms of its established pattern of social relations and cultural biases), the influences that shaped cultural change, the subsequent effects of those changes, and the implications for US-China relations, in particular. China remains a mystery to many US policy makers and military planners. Yet through careful analysis of China's cultural experience, the

United States may find better understanding that will lead to improved international relations and strategic partnering.

Nature of China's Culture: Past and Present

One of the remarkable features of Chinese culture is that it is based on the oldest continuing cultural tradition in the world and yet, as John King Fairbank notes, recent archeological studies show that "distinctive features of Chinese life today, such as autocratic government, come down directly from pre-historic times."[37] These "distinctive features" were the cultural biases and patterns of social relations that developed during China's early period in the form of a collective, highly structured social system that solved the problem of how best to govern and maintain the security and prosperity of a large, diverse agrarian populace. Four examples of China's bias toward a high-group and high-grid way of life that emerged early in its history were the emphasis on kinship relations, the role and legitimization of patriarchal authority, the Confucianist concept of bureaucratic governance, and the system of tribute.

Archeological evidence indicates that as early as the Neolithic age (some 12,000 years ago), when the spread of agricultural communities began in China, villagers organized themselves in clustered kinship units, grouped to maximize their ability to survive by reaping the most from the limited cultivable land available.[38] Survival under oftentimes harsh and unpredictable conditions required family members and neighbors to work closely together, and this strong reliance on each other "accustomed the Chinese people to a collective life in which the group normally dominates the individual."[39] The sense of collectivism was further reinforced during the dynastic age (circa 221 B.C.) when a "legal system of mutual responsibility" was enforced.[40] This system held all family members and their neighbors accountable for one another, strengthening the collective bias and maintaining order by impelling people to keep an eye on one another.[41]

Not only did the agrarian-based family tradition establish a strong collective bias in Chinese culture, it was also the basis for China's autocratic social structure (i.e., high-grid bias). As Fairbank notes, the family was the social unit led by the patriarch.[42] Within the traditional family group, age dominated youth and men dominated women. Stability in the family group was maintained by the high value placed on respect for one's place and the harmony of working within the established social order.

As contact between the early farming villages grew, kinship networks and alliances created an opportunity for broader gov-ernment along a central family line. Eventually, the communi-ties evolved into dynasties, ruled by a patriarchal emperor. The problem of how to ensure the legitimate authority of the ruling family was solved through the concept of heaven's mandate. [43] According to this central cultural belief, the patriarch of the state, while at the top of the human order of society, held a middle position in the hierarchy of heaven and earth, and main-tained legitimate authority over the Chung Kuo (Middle King-dom) through heaven's conferred mandate to rule.

These early traditions of collectivism and the strict patterns of social relations necessary to support the hierarchical system were reinforced with the rise of Confucianism, in the second century B.C., as the central ideology of the Chinese way of life. For example, Confucianism postulated that "a true civilization was to be achieved under the leadership of an elite educated in its ideals and dedicated to the service of those under them." [44] This belief allowed the formation of a well-organized bureauc-racy to manage a growing population (swarming to over 53 mil-lion by the second century B.C.). Membership in the elite group at the top of the bureaucracy was available only to the wealthy and literate, thus restricting officialdom to those at the top of the social strata. Although Confucianist belief in China changed over the centuries, the bureaucracy persisted as a powerful means of reinforcing the high-grid and high-group central autocracy, and it created a formidable governmental hierarchy highly effective in managing a huge mass of people.

Confucianism also helped to establish China's original sys-tem of foreign policy—a system based on an institution of trib-ute. The tributary system was rooted in China's belief that its culture was not only the most viable way of life for its people, but that it also was superior to other forms of civilization. [45] According to Mark Borthwick, China's ancient leaders believed "the rest of the world was culturally inferior, inhabited by bar-barians whose natural inclination would be to seek favorable relations with [their country]." [46] Thus, any foreigners wishing access to China were required to bring tribute to the emperor by "kowtowing" before him and acknowledging him as the center of all civilization.[47] This system provided a setting for foreign trade. More important, it preserved the prestige of the empire and reinforced an ethnocentric view that the Middle Kingdom was mankind's only true civilization.

As this analytical review of China's early history demonstrates, China's historical culture, in terms of the group-grid typology, was strongly hierarchical. This way of life remained viable for centuries by virtue of the compatibility of biases and social patterns that manifested themselves in such early traditions as the importance of familial bonds and the role and legitimization of patriarchal authority in the hierarchy of heaven and earth. Confucianist orthodoxy further reinforced the culture through its emphasis on bureaucratic governance and a system of tribute that strengthened China's view of the preeminence of its way of life over other forms of civilization.

The Chinese belief in the viability and superiority of its ancient hierarchical culture was strongly challenged with the arrival of British trade ships at the beginning of the nineteenth century.[48] A "clash of civilizations"[49] occurred when the British found the Chinese tributary system intolerable. China, faced with the destabilizing effects of an exploding population and the demoralization that emerged from a growing demand for British-supplied opium, "tried to coerce the British within the framework of the outworn tribute system."[50] The result was the Opium War in which "the British thought themselves the righteous champions of modern (Western) civilization over Chinese backwardness."[51] According to Fairbank, British trade pressure and the war that followed set a dangerous precedent for Western relations with China, "for the British were demanding that China join the international order according to Western rules."[52] Nevertheless, for the first time in three thousand years, China's culture was severely challenged by external pressure and, as Douglas's group-grid theory indicates, was confronted with the question of its own viability and need to change.

For the next century, Western expansion caused many Chinese to question the compatibility of old solutions with the new problems of security and prosperity in a changing world. "In every sphere of social activity, the old order was challenged, attacked, undermined, or overwhelmed by a complex series of processes—political, economic, social, ideological, cultural—all set in motion by the penetration of an alien and more powerful society."[53] Western missionaries preaching egalitarianism, individualism, and democracy presented new ideas that undermined the high-group and high-grid orientation of the Confucianist way of life and created a rising undercurrent of social unrest against the imperial regime.[54] By 1900 the imperial institution came under full attack by Chinese revolutionaries who denounced the monarchy as the source of China's weakness and incapacity to deal with modern challenges.

Note that Western expansion was merely the trigger that caused the Chinese to question the viability of their culture. As pointed out earlier, cultural change occurs when "people realize that certain old ways of doing things do not work any more."[55] Thus, culture change may be influenced by an external source but the constituent members of the culture carry it out. According to Fairbank, "The Chinese in the nineteenth century were undone by the very factors that had given them such early success in the art of government."[56] The strict pattern of social relations maintained via a system of central authority and orthodoxy, and the collectivist bias that emphasized responsibility to and superiority of the empire had allowed the ancient Chinese to solve one problem of stability after another. "When the West broke in and presented new problems, the old solutions were produced and tried again, but they would not work."[57] Loyalty demanded by the ancient Chinese way of life was not to the leadership or the nation-state (indeed, the dynasties and their ruling leaders were prone to change under the theory of heaven's mandate).[58] Instead loyalty was "to the ancient culture and institutions. When China's ancient culture proved inadequate to deal with modern challenges, [it lost its viability] and the Chinese were left without a focus."[59]

By the first quarter of the twentieth century, with the viability of its hierarchical way of life questioned, China was struggling for cultural solutions to meet the new challenges to its security and prosperity. As indicated by Douglas's research on the nature of cultural change, China was now being pulled in at least three divergent directions along the dimensions of the group-grid construct. Western influences favoring greater individualism, emancipation of women, and technological progress continued to pull the Chinese way of life away from its high-grid and high-group orientation. Meanwhile, a new nationalism arose as patriotic Chinese youth sought to revive the power of central authority and maintain the hierarchy.[60] At the same time, "with no monarchic system to guide them, the swollen numbers of peasantry were living precariously" in a fatalistic state, and growing more and more concerned.[61] These pressures continued to bring into question the ancient way of life while new ways of life, based on different cultural biases and social patterns, struggled to emerge.

Eventually, two competing, organized movements for revolution arose, and while both offered the promise of an alternative way of life to better meet the demands of the current environment, neither could break through the underlying assumptions inherent in the traditional hierarchic culture. Sun Yat-sen and his Kuomintang Nationalist movement offered the promise of "Nationalism, People's Rights or Democracy, and People's Livelihood" and implied a move toward greater individualism.[62] The Chinese Communist Party (CCP) meanwhile pursued a Marxist-Leninist inspired drive toward socialism, or increased egalitarianism.

The thrust toward greater democracy under the Nationalist movement failed when the Kuomintang "developed no higher aim than the preservation of [its own] power" and lost the opportunity to be a powerful force of social change.[63] Nationalist leaders set up a centralized bureaucratic regime much like that of the ancient dynasties, managed by an official elite "who feathered their private nests in the domination of industry and finance."[64] As Fairbank observes, "the Kuomintang had little desire for change once they were in power and instead stoked the existing class system to keep them in power and, in essence, keep the tradition of [hierarchy] in place."[65]

The Chinese Communists "offered the down-trodden peasants at the bottom of the hierarchical system [the most] hope of economic betterment,"[66] and a way out of the fatalistic state they had found themselves in since the decline of the aristocracy. Searching for a viable means to support China's collapsed rural society, Mao Tse-tung and his revolutionaries idealized an egalitarian brotherhood that would free the people from the traditional hierarchic evils of "the four olds—old ideas, old habits, old customs, old culture."[67] Yet, despite the egalitarian fervor, the communist revolution could not free China from its Confucianist past. While proclaiming to be laboring

for the welfare of the people as a whole, the Communists continued to reinforce the basic Confucianist system of bureaucracy
with its need for an elite ruling body educated in the central
ideology and dedicated to the service of the masses.[68] Additionally,
just as ancient Chinese tradition emphasized the family structure
as the basic societal pattern, the CCP "built an even tighter political family for politicizing culture, law, economics and private
life,"[69] ordered by a strict hierarchical authority that espoused
Marxism as its new central orthodoxy. The egalitarian ideal was
never achieved as the Communists reorganized China under a
totalitarian polity and a command economy, pulling China back
toward the age-old high-grid and high-group way of life. Perhaps,
as Fairbank states, China realized it would have to "remain some
kind of bureaucratic state, essentially inward looking (because of
the sheer mass and growing complexity of the body politic), and
concerned with social order more than growth."[70]

Unable to compete politically or economically with the free-
market world, the overplanned and overcentralized Chinese Communist system could not fulfill its promise of economic betterment.[71] Thus, by the end of the Maoist era, the Chinese way of life
again came under attack, faced with divergent internal pressures
for cultural change. As Thompson, Ellis, and Wildavsky observe,
"the outcome of the Maoist era was so at odds with the promise,
that it enabled rival [hierarchical and individualist] ways of life to
attract adherents and gain political power."[72] Some 150 years after
the fall of the aristocracy, China was still struggling to reconcile
itself to the hierarchical traditions that had given it so much
strength in the past, while at the same time hoping to find a viable
means to ensure its security and prosperity in the current environment.

When Deng Xiaoping came into power in 1978, his reforms
attempted, for the first time, to balance China's deep-set hierarchic orientation with the promise of more liberalized structures
to support national security and prosperity. While a product of
China's totalitarian regime, Deng realized that the only way to
restore China to its rightful and respected position of greatness
was through economic strength to be realized by a change in
favor of a more liberal, individualistic way of life, at least from
an economic point of view. As a result, he instituted sweeping
agricultural reform, urban economic commercialization, and a
new "open policy" toward foreign trade, which enabled China to

"double the size of its economy, raise living standards two to three times and join the world economy for the first time." [73]

As Douglas's group-grid theory predicts, however, cultural change and the subsequent positive results achieved through the Deng reforms prompted dangerous destabilizing tensions. Turbulent economic cycles, corruption, and varied stresses produced by rapid social change were the inevitable outcome of a society transitioning to support greater economic growth. Entrepreneurial impulses unleashed by decentralization and commercialization raised hopes for more local autonomy (i.e., greater individualism), higher living standards, and greater pluralism. Meanwhile, rising inflation heightened fears of a shift toward increased fatalism for those less privileged, ambitious, or lucky in the game of free market economics. Tensions on each side of the change were directed at the central leadership as a tide of cynicism (fostered by newly sophisticated urbanites) rose against what was perceived as a corrupt, ineffective officialdom standing on an irrelevant ideology.

The boiling point of all of the social, economic, and political tension was reached with the Tiananmen crisis in 1989, the roots of which "can be found in a mixture of the reform's successes and shortcomings." [74] Ronald N. Montaperto offers this explanation: "Deng's open policy gave China the opportunity to compare itself with the non-Chinese world, and the reform policies brought a new stress on incentive and ambition." [75] At the same time, the reforms produced "unsettling effects of inflation and corruption." [76] Between the new fears and opportunities, the current highly authoritarian way of life was called into question. A serious vacuum of values arose, much like the void created by the decline of imperial autocracy more than 150 years earlier, [77] and the outcome was a standoff between the ardent representatives of two divergent ways of life.

While A. Doak Barnett asserts, "the decision to suppress the demonstrations with military force was a tragic failure of leadership," in many ways it was a predictable response when one considers the cultural factors described earlier in this paper. [78] First, "China's leaders have viewed their mandate to govern and the role of the state in terms that are as old as China itself." [79] To allow any type of rebellion to occur which could threaten domestic stability would bring into question the ruling party's mandate to govern and, thus, its legitimate authority. Second, as the research for this paper has shown, China's leaders have always been concerned with the potential for chaos given the sheer size of its population. To control such a huge and diverse mass of people, some form of collectivist, highly structured governance has been the system of choice for centuries. Third, in putting down the demonstration, the Deng government relied on the age-old Chinese bias that supports suppressing individualism in favor of the collective good. The government knew the population was vulnerable to pressures to conform and acquiesce, and it, therefore, could and did take firm action.

Nevertheless, the tense frustrations and desires that grew out of the Deng reforms shook the most basic foundational beliefs of China's still hierarchical way of life—perhaps more violently than ever before. Once again, the viability of the existing way of life had been brought into question, and in the aftermath of Tiananmen, strong undercurrents calling for a new way of life persisted and continue today.

In today's China, some leaders seem prepared to proceed cautiously with gradual change, and assert that even now, China has moved "from an extreme form of Maoist totalitarianism to a much looser, and in some respects partially liberalized form of authoritarianism."[80] However many Chinese, both inside and outside the power structure, still cling to the cultural traditions that give highest priority to the need to preserve stability and prevent social disorder.

While much of the above appears promising for those in favor of increased, albeit gradual liberalization in China, deeply rooted collectivism and social stratification have existed for centuries, have survived violent periods of change over the last two hundred years, and remain strong influences in the Chinese way of life. The historical analysis in this section provides US policy makers and military planners with a foundation from which they can begin to assess China's potential response to today's strategic challenges and United States efforts to shape China's role in the international environment. More specific recommendations for how the United States should proceed in dealing with China as it explores future cultural change in light of its long-standing traditions follow.

Analyzing US-China Relations
through a Cultural Lens

The United States has identified three core objectives in its National Security Strategy that it wishes to pursue in the international environment: enhanced security, economic prosperity, and promotion of democracy abroad. China's booming economy, increasing modernization, and large population (creating a potentially strong market for US products) make effective international relations with China important to the achievement of each of these objectives. Therefore, the United States is pursuing a strategy of peacetime engagement with China in the hope of facilitating "a stable, open, prosperous People's Republic of China (PRC) that assumes its responsibilities for building a more peaceful world."[81]

Developing successful peacetime engagement strategies with China depends on the ability of the United States to apply an understanding of culture and how culturally established mind-sets affect diplomatic and military planning efforts. Earlier in this paper, the author showed that these mind-sets, based on the established cultural biases and patterns of social relations, influence the way people of different cultures view the world and solve the problems presented to them. The historical analysis revealed the cultural lens through which China views the world, providing US policy makers and military planners with a better sense of the cultural prescriptions that have shaped China's way of life, its challenges with culture change, and its strategies for security and prosperity. The author now applies this understanding by analyzing how culture affects current US-China relations, particularly with regard to the issue of broader democratization in China and the implications for long-term strategic cooperation.

Historians and political analysts generally agree that US-China relations have been hindered by a lack of consistency and "punctuated by one crisis after another."[82] Susan M. Puska asserts that the inconsistent nature of US-China relations, reflected as a "boom-bust paradigm," is based on a deep "perceptual gap" caused by "philosophical and cultural differences, historical experiences and ideological differences."[83] As discussed earlier, China's highly collectivist and structured way of life, reinforced by centuries of experience, has inculcated certain values and beliefs many Chinese continue to hold relevant and viable—despite internal tensions that have recently moved China gradually toward more liberal preferences. The American experience, on the other hand, has instilled in most Americans a much more individualistic worldview biased toward liberaliza-tion in all facets of society and government. These fundamen-tally different perspectives shape fundamentally different solu-tions to the common problems of security and prosperity and "help explain why miscommunication often arises between China and the US."[84]

Long-term strategic cooperation with China requires that the United States understand how these cultural differences pre-sent the potential for misperception and dangerous miscalcula-tions in policy. Moreover, US leaders must factor these differ-ences into cooperative plans for every realm of engagement with China. The question of increased democratization in China is a critical issue in which cultural differences may dangerously cloud successful strategic cooperation.

China's powerful hierarchic tradition demands that its lead-ers continue to resist pressures for democratization, giving "highest priority . . . to the need to preserve political stability and prevent major social and political disorders,"[85] despite pro-found change in many facets of Chinese society over the last two decades. While many Chinese leaders "seem prepared to proceed cautiously . . . with gradual change,"[86] broad democra-tization is extremely "problematic for China's leaders who see it as a direct . . . threat to [national stability] that could potentially throw the country into the chaos of internal revolution."[87] This apparent incongruity among China's leadership regarding de-mocratization also exists in other influential circles of Chinese society. Thomas A. Metzgar states that "despite the Tiananmen demonstrations in 1989, there is not a clear dichotomy today among many Chinese intellectuals between the existing party line and the democracy movement."[88] He cites the writings of one of China's most prominent intellectuals, Li Tse-hou, noting that Li appears to stride both camps, affirming Maoist ideals while persistently supporting the democratic values of equality and freedom.[89] This ambivalence gets at the crux of China's cultural dilemma as it struggles to reconcile its bias towards collectivism and social control with the pressures for greater democratization without causing the country to disintegrate into chaos.

It is also important to note that China's desire to curb democ-ratization and willingness to use coercion in the process (as evidence at Tiananmen Square and via the continued imprison-ment and harsh treatment of political dissidents) are consistent with the underlying beliefs of its hierarchic culture. According to Sun-Ki Chai and Aaron Wildavsky in their application of the Douglas group-grid model to predict the causes of political vio-lence, hierarchists "see anyone who opposes the hierarchy as a threat to the group and to themselves [and] are likely to resort to coercion to control recalcitrant behavior."[90]

To US observers, these ambivalent and seemingly irrational domestic policies in China are confusing and, in many ways, diametrically opposed to the American cultural mind-set. Ac-cording to Douglas's group-grid model, the American way of life is oriented toward a much more individualistic view of the world. As such, American culture emphasizes "inalienable" and "self-evident" rights to "life, liberty, and the pursuit of happi-ness" as universal truths. Many Americans, therefore, have dif-ficulty understanding China's view on human rights, "based more on the collective good than on the rights of the individ-ual."[91] Additionally, Geert H. Hofstede notes that "individualist societies not only practice individualism, but they also consider it superior to other forms of [culture]."[92] Thus, Americans see the spread of their individualist values (e.g., democracy and liberty for all) as part of their "Manifest Destiny" and critical to US security and prosperity.[93] As a result, US National Security Strategy has made the promotion of democracy and free-market economies around the world one of its core objectives.

Given the dangerous cultural gap with regard to democratiza-tion, how then should the United States proceed in developing effective bilateral relations with China in a way that supports the concerns and goals of both countries? First, Seymour Mar-tin Lipset argues the United States must recognize that "press-ing for immediate democratization is not necessarily the most effective way to democratize, and that . . . in some cases nonde-mocratic, authoritarian rule may be advisable during periods of transition during which the social requisites of democratization can be further realized."[94] Indeed this seems to be the prevailing attitude among many today in China. As Barnett notes, "most who favor political change [in China] hope for an incremental

process of political liberalization leading in a democratic direc -
tion."[95]

Additionally, the United States must realize that other exam -
ples of democratization in East Asia, while very different from
the American model, may be much more applicable to China.
Barnett suggests, "the Taiwan and South Korean models, where
the progression from rapid economic growth to major social
change to the start of real democratization took two to three
decades, seem most relevant to China."[96] Another relevant
model is Singapore whose founding leader built a stable, or -
derly, and highly prosperous system based on a "benevolent
democratized authoritarianism."[97] As discussed earlier, the no -
tion of an incremental approach to cultural change as a way to
avoid the potentially destabilizing and violent consequences of
change is consistent with Douglas's group-grid theory. Ellis and
Coyle, remarking on the group-grid concept, state that "rather
than expecting dramatic changes when someone passes
through no-man's land from one culture to another, [one] can
recognize that the passage may involve only a series of modest
incremental shifts in the weighting of preferences."[98] Most important, the United States must exercise caution and open-
mindedness in its efforts to shape the international environ -
ment, recognizing that, to China's leaders, the spread of
Western values "is seen as a threat to China and to things
Chinese."[99] The Opium War occurred because the "British [de -
manded] China join the international order according to West -
ern rules."[100] This triggered a series of turbulent changes in
China that led to the downfall of the ancient empire and seri -
ously challenged the hierarchical way of life. As a result, the
Chinese believe "China has experienced 'a century of humili -
ation' at the hands of Western powers."[101] This belief system
causes many Chinese leaders to "be hypersensitive to issues of
national sovereignty or anything that might appear to be inter -
ference in China's internal affairs."[102]

Herein lies the great potential for conflict and miscalculations
in policy between the United States and China regarding de -
mocratization. As Alastair Johnston warns, while many schol -
ars have persistently argued that "China's strategic culture is
essentially nonthreatening," China believes, nevertheless, that
"the best way of dealing with security threats is to eliminate
them through the use of force."[103] American military planners

and policy makers must carefully consider the cultural differences between the United States and China regarding such issues as democratization. It is unclear just how far China will go
with democratization, but the process is certain to be ap-
proached slowly and cautiously. China's form of democratization will be molded by its own biases and traditions, and will
have the most chance of success when influenced, not from an
external source, but from "changes in the perceptions and prac-
tices of the Chinese people themselves."[104]

While the potential for conflict over such issues as democratization exists, most military observers in Asia and the United
States believe that "it will take China at least ten years before
they can acquire enough military power to threaten US interests."[105] An effective strategy for peacetime engagement holds
the promise of not only deterring future conflict but also of
securing a long-term strategic partnership between the United
States and China. Achieving this partnership requires that US
leaders and planners strive to overcome the boom-bust paradigm of inconsistent relations with China and establish a coher-
ent and articulate strategy that addresses cultural differences
and their effect on strategic cooperation.

Conclusion

The avoidance of hostilities between any two parties lies in the
ability of each to develop and sustain a mutual understanding of
and respect for the other's challenges and aspirations. An understanding of cultural theory and its implications for international
relations is an important resource for US leadership in formulat-
ing the types of exchanges and dialogues that will lead to constructive partnering and resolution of differences.

In this paper, the author explains the important role that
culture plays in domestic and international relations. The use of
the group-grid typology model shows how certain ways of life can
differ from others and illustrates the tensions inherent in any
transition from one way of life to another. The author also applies this model to frame an analysis of China's culture, the
transitional challenges that have shaped China's way of life over
the last two hundred years, and the impact of culture on US-
China relations and prospects for future strategic cooperation.

In today's dynamic strategic environment, with the explosion of global communications, new ideas are being promulgated literally at the speed of light. The rapid-fire exchange of ideas inevitably will drive new expectations, hopes, and fears as many cultures grapple with their existing biases and patterns of social relations in light of the new opportunities presented from other worldviews. China stands at the forefront of this dilemma, at-tempting to adapt its traditional way of life to these opportuni-ties while preserving its security and prosperity.

With a 1.4 billion population, an economy that has grown 7 to 9 percent annually, nuclear power, and a modernizing mili-tary force, China is critically important to US National Security Strategy and National Military Strategy. Building a strong stra-tegic partnership with China demands that the United States exert a constructive influence on China's development by seek-ing first to understand the powerful nature of China's ancient cultural traditions and the challenges faced by Chinese leaders as their country transitions. Armed with this understanding, US policy makers and military planners will be more effective in building strong bilateral communications, expanding trade and security links, and assisting in China's full integration as a key leader in the international community.

Notes

1. Glen Fisher, Mindsets: The Role of Culture and Perception in International Relations (Yarmouth, Maine: Intercultural Press, 1988), 1.

2. Ibid.

3. Ibid.

4. Joint Chiefs of Staff, National Military Strategy of the United States of America: Shape, Respond, Prepare Now: A Military Strategy for a New Era (Washington, D.C.: Joint Chiefs of Staff, 1997), 1.

5. Paul M. Belbutowski, "The Strategic Implications of Cultures in Conflict," Parameters 26, no. 1 (Spring 1996): 34.

6. Jack S. Levy, "Misperception and the Causes of War: Theoretical Linkages and Analytical Problems," World Politics 36, no. 1 (October 1983): 99.

7. Fons Trompenaar, Riding the Waves of Culture (Chicago: Irwin Publish-ing, 1994), 6.

8. Ibid., 7.

9. Ibid.

10. Ibid., 25.

11. Edgar Schein, "What Is Culture," in Reframing Organizational Culture, ed. Peter J. Frost et al. (Newbury Park, Calif.: Sage Publications, 1991), 252.

12. Richard J. Ellis and Dennis J. Coyle, Politics, Policy and Culture (Boul-der, Colo.: Westview Press, 1994), 2. The use of the term cultural theory in this

paper is based on the argument presented by Richard Ellis and Dennis Coyle in the introduction to their book, Politics, Policy and Culture. Ellis and Coyle assert that cultural theory should "create measures of culture that allow for compari - sons across time and space and relate values and beliefs to social relations and institutions. Fundamental to this method is the assumption that it is through the mundane encounters of everyday life that we develop our values and beliefs and learn how our aspirations . . . are interrelated with our preferences about social institutions and organizations."

13. Michael Thompson, Richard Ellis, and Aaron Wildavsky, Cultural Theory (Boulder, Colo.: Westview Press, 1990), 1. The authors state that American anthropologists largely agree with this inclusive concept and refer readers to Ruth Benedict, Patterns of Culture (Boston: Houghton Mifflin, 1934).

14. Thompson, Ellis, and Wildavsky, 1.

15. Trompenaar, 24.

16. Thompson, Ellis, and Wildavsky, 2.

17. Clifford Geertz, The Interpretation of Cultures: Selected Essays (New York: Basic Books, 1973), 27.

18. Belbutowski, 32.

19. Trompenaar, 29. Geert H. Hofstede supports this assertion in his book, Cultures and Organizations: Software of the Mind (New York: McGraw-Hill, 1997), 13. Hofstede cites the work of Ruth Benedict, Margaret Meade, Alex Inkeles, and David Levinson as important contributors to this idea.

20. Thompson, Ellis, and Wildavsky, 5.

21. Mary Douglas, "Cultural Bias," in In the Active Voice, ed. Mary Douglas (London: Routledge and Kegan Paul, 1982), 191.

22. Ibid., 203.

23. Thompson, Ellis, and Wildavsky, 6.

24. Ibid., 3.

25. Ibid., 6.

26. Ibid., 7.

27. Geertz, 27.

28. Trompenaar, 25.

29. Thompson, Ellis, and Wildavsky, 3.

30. Ibid., 69.

31. Ibid.

32. Douglas, 191.

33. John King Fairbank, China Perceived: Images and Policies in Chinese-American Relations (New York: Alfred A. Knopf Publishers, 1974), 7.

34. A. Doak Barnett, US China Policy—Building a New Consensus (Washington, D.C.: Center for Strategic and International Studies, 1994), 7.

35. Ibid., 44.

36. Ibid., 40.

37. John King Fairbank, China: A New History (Cambridge, Mass.: Belknap Press, 1992), 25.

38. Ibid., 32.

39. Ibid., 17.

40. John King Fairbank, China: The People's Middle Kingdom and the U.S.A. (Cambridge, Mass.: Belknap Press, 1967), 7.

41. Ibid.

42. Fairbank, China: A New History, 18.

43. Yosef Lapid and Friedrich Kratochwil, eds., The Return of Culture and Identity in IR Theory (Boulder, Colo.: Lynne Rienner Publishers, 1996), 30.

44. Kenneth Scott Latourette, The Chinese: Their History and Culture (New York: Macmillian, 1964), 400.

45. Lapid and Kratochwil, 28. This idea is also found in Mark Borthwick, Pacific Century: The Emergence of Modern Pacific Asia (Boulder, Colo.: Westview Press, 1996), 30.

46. Borthwick, 30.

47. Fairbank, China: The People's Middle Kingdom and the U.S.A., 8.

48. Ibid., 10.

49. Samuel Huntington, "The Clash of Civilizations?" in Strategic Environment, vol. 4, eds. Gwen Story and Eva Hensley (Maxwell AFB, Ala.: Air Command and Staff College, October 1997), 48.

50. Ibid.

51. Ibid.

52. Ibid.

53. Ssu-yu Teng and John K. Fairbank, China's Response to the West: A Documentary Survey 1839–1923 (Cambridge, Mass.: Harvard University Press, 1954), 1.

54. Fairbank, China: The People's Middle Kingdom and the U.S.A., 11. "The violent rebellions of 1850 in which Chinese peasants mobilized against the Peking dynasty highlighted the threat to the Chinese Confucian way of life."

55. Trompenaar, 25.

56. Fairbank, China: The People's Middle Kingdom and the U.S.A., 13.

57. Ibid.

58. Ibid.

59. Ibid.

60. Ibid., 37.

61. Ibid.

62. Fairbank, China: A New History, 281.

63. Ibid., 288.

64. Ibid., 289.

65. Fairbank, China Perceived, 20.

66. Ibid.

67. Fairbank, China: The People's Middle Kingdom and the U.S.A., viii.

68. Borthwick, 404. Under the Communist Party's 1950–1953 Land Reform Movement, some 40 percent of China's cultivated land changed hands as land-lords were deposed and property was redistributed to peasantry associations that were consolidated under party control. By 1956, "over 90% of all rural families had been organized into about 700,000 higher level Agricultural Producer Cooperatives (APC). Peasants turned over the land and tools to the collective, receiving pay in the form of work points."

69. Ronald N. Montaperto, "China Prepares for the Future: The Challenges for the United States," in The Future of US-China Relations (Washington, D.C.: Center for Strategic and International Studies, September 1992), 32.

70. Fairbank, China Perceived, 58.

71. Fairbank, China: The People's Middle Kingdom and the U.S.A., xi.

72. Thompson, Ellis, and Wildavsky, 88.

73. Barnett, 6.

74. Montaperto, 32.

75. Ibid.

76. Ibid.

77. Ibid.

78. Barnett, 38.

79. Borthwick, 403.

80. Barnett, 38.

81. A National Security Strategy for a New Century (Washington, D.C.: White House, October 1998), 43.

82. Susan M. Puska, "New Century, Old Thinking: The Dangers of Perceptual Gap in US-China Relations" (Carlisle Barracks, Pa.: US Army War College, Strategic Studies Institute, 10 August 1998), 1.

83. Ibid., 2.

84. Ibid., 7.

85. Barnett, 39.

86. Ibid.

87. Puska, 12.

88. Thomas A. Metzgar, "The US Quest for Morality in Foreign Policy and the Issue of Chinese Democratization," in Greater China and US Foreign Policy: The Choice between Confrontation and Mutual Respect, eds. Thomas A. Metzgar and Ramon H. Myers (Stanford, Calif.: Hoover Institute Press, 1996), 96.

89. Ibid.

90. Sun-Ki Chai and Aaron Wildavsky, "Culture, Rationality and Violence," in Politics, Policy and Culture, eds. Richard J. Ellis and Dennis J. Coyle (Boulder, Colo.: Westview Press, 1994), 170.

91. Puska, 12.

92. Hofstede, 71.

93. Puska, 7.

94. Summarization of Seymour Martin Lipset in his 1993 presidential address to the American Sociological Association, quoted in Metzgar, 87.

95. Barnett, 40.

96. Ibid.

97. Ibid.

98. Ellis and Coyle, 220.

99. Puska, 9.

100. Fairbank, China: The People's Middle Kingdom and the U.S.A., 10.

101. Kim R. Holmes and James J. Przystup, eds., Between Diplomacy and Deterrence: Strategies for US Relations with China (Washington, D.C.: Heritage Foundation, 1997), 24.

102. Ibid.

103. Alastair I. Johnston, Cultural Realism: Strategic Culture and Grand Strategy in Chinese History (Princeton, N.J.: Princeton University Press, 1995), 214.

104. Nancy Bernkopf Tucker, "A Precarious Balance: Clinton and China," Current History, September 1998, 244.

105. Richard Halloran, "China: Restoring the Middle Kingdom," Parameters 28, no. 2 (Summer 1998): 68.